Sanjeev Kapoor

TEATIME TREATS

In association with Alyona Kapoor

Popular Prakashan
www.popularprakashan.com

Published by
POPULAR PRAKASHAN PVT. LTD.
301, Mahalaxmi Chambers
22, Bhulabhai Desai Road
Mumbai - 400 026
for Khana Khazana Publications Pvt. Ltd.

First Published 2016

(4433)
ISBN: 978-81-7991-874-6

Design: Anjali Sawant

PRINTED IN INDIA
by Saurabh Printers (P) Ltd.
Plot No. 67 A-68, Ecotech, Ext. I
Kasna, Greater Noida-201306 (U.P)

Author's Note

Teatime is incomplete without teatime treats. 'Teatime Treats' is a compilation of healthy and quick recipes with everyday ingredients. Enjoy the Seafood Spring Rolls or Maddur Vade, Crispy Potato Fingers or Bhakarvadi, Chocolate Èclairs or Steamed Date Buns and gulp it all down with cups of steaming hot tea or Chocolate Coffee.

All the recipes serve four portions. There are some that can be made in bulk and stored in airtight tins to be had anytime while there are some that taste best when served hot, but they are all equally enjoyable. So make them, serve them to your family and friends and you are sure to feel gratified when you see their faces lit up with satiated smiles.

Happy Cooking!

Contents

Non-Vegetarian Snacks and Starters

Desserts

Strawberry Granita

1 cup strawberry crush
1 cup orange juice
2 tablespoons lemon juice
4 strawberries, sliced
A few sprigs of fresh mint
5 cups crushed ice

- Process strawberry crush, orange juice, lemon juice and crushed ice well.
- Pour into stemmed glasses and serve, decorated with strawberry slices and mint sprigs.

Chef's Tip: You can add chopped strawberries to the mixture and freeze it for an ice-cold slushy granita.

Coffee Ambrosia

3 cups milk

4 teaspoons instant coffee powder

4 tablespoons sugar

4 scoops vanilla ice cream

4 tablespoons advocaat (liqueur)

- Heat the milk and set aside. To make the coffee, combine the coffee powder and sugar in a large bowl. Add two to three tablespoons of water and whisk for six to eight minutes till the mixture changes colour and turns creamy.
- Pour the mixture into four large cups. Strain the milk and pour into the cups till three-fourth full and stir gently. Gently place a scoop of ice cream on the coffee in each cup. Drizzle a tablespoon of advocaat over the ice cream and serve immediately.

Note: *Dinner is over and your guests are replete. Bring on one more surprise with this advocaat-laced delight that is truly creamy and soothing. It can be served warm without the ice cream.*

Kahwa

1 teaspoon kahwa tea leaves, crushed
2 green cardamoms
2 inches cinnamon
3 teaspoons sugar
2-3 saffron threads (optional)
4-5 almonds, finely crushed

- Pound cardamoms and cinnamon to a powder.
- Pour three cups of water into a non-stick pan; add crushed kahwa tea leaves, cardamom-cinnamon powder, sugar and saffron and bring to a boil.
- Boil for five to six minutes, or till the tea turns a pale gold. Strain into teacups.
- Sprinkle the almonds on top and serve hot.

Maddur Vade

½ cup semolina

½ cup rice flour

½ cup refined flour

5 green chillies, chopped

2 onions, chopped

2 tablespoons chopped fresh coriander

3 tablespoons melted ghee

Salt to taste

Oil for deep-frying

- Mix together all the ingredients except oil, adding a very little water, and make a stiff dough.
- To make each vada, place a ladleful of dough on the palm of one hand and flatten it with the other hand.
- Heat sufficient oil in a kadai and deep-fry the vade, a few at a time, until golden brown and crisp. Drain on absorbent paper.
- Serve hot or cold with any chutney.

Kanchipuram Idli

1 cup rice

½ cup skinless split black gram

¾ teaspoon fenugreek seeds

1 teaspoon turmeric powder

20-25 black peppercorns

2 teaspoons split Bengal gram

A pinch of asafoetida

1 cup yogurt

½ cup pure ghee

Salt to taste

A few tender banana leaves

- Soak the rice and split black gram along with the fenugreek seeds for three to four hours. Drain and grind to a smooth paste with sufficient water to make a thick batter.
- Add the turmeric powder, peppercorns, split Bengal gram, asafoetida, yogurt, ghee and salt. Mix well and leave to ferment overnight, or for at least six hours.

- Whip the batter and adjust the consistency. The batter should be fairly thick. Heat sufficient water in a steamer. Line the idli moulds with the banana leaves and pour the batter into them.
- Place in the steamer and steam for about twenty minutes or till done. Serve with coconut chutney and sambhar.

Mirchi Bhajiya

8 large chillies, slit and seeded

1 cup gram flour

1 teaspoon baking powder

½ teaspoon asafoetida

1 teaspoon red chilli powder

Salt to taste

1 tablespoon oil + for deep-frying

½ teaspoon mustard seeds

4-5 garlic cloves, crushed

¼ teaspoon turmeric powder

2 large potatoes, boiled and mashed

- Whisk the gram flour, baking powder, asafoetida, chilli powder and salt with approximately one cup of water in a deep bowl to make a smooth batter. Set aside for about ten minutes.
- To make the filling, heat one tablespoon of oil in a non-stick pan and add the mustard seeds. When they begin to splutter add the crushed garlic and sauté on medium heat till fragrant. Add the turmeric powder and the mashed potatoes and mix well. Add the salt and mix. Remove from heat and set aside to cool.
- Divide the mixture into eight equal portions and stuff each chilli with a portion of the filling.
- Heat sufficient oil in a kadai. Dip the chillies in the gram flour batter and deep-fry till golden and crisp. Drain on absorbent paper. Serve hot.

Chef's Tip: Select large-sized green chillies for this recipe. It will not only give it a nice definite shape but also would not be very spicy.

Fried Mozzarella

400 grams mozzarella cheese

2 eggs

½ cup refined flour

Salt to taste

¼ teaspoon peppercorns, crushed

1 cup breadcrumbs

Oil for deep-frying

A few sprigs parsley

- Cut the mozzarella cheese into one-inch squares with half-inch thickness. Gently pat off any excess moisture with kitchen paper.
- Mix the eggs lightly and keep aside.
- Season the flour with salt and freshly crushed peppercorns.
- Spread the seasoned flour on one plate and breadcrumbs on another plate.
- Press the cheese slices into the flour, coating them evenly with a thin layer of flour. Shake off the excess flour.

- Dip them into the egg, then roll them in breadcrumbs. Repeat this process once.
- Heat sufficient oil in a kadai or wok to a smoking point and deep-fry the cheese slices until golden brown. Drain onto an absorbent kitchen paper.
- Serve hot immediately (as mozzarella has a tendency of melting fast) garnished with sprigs of parsley.

Herb and Onion Bread

1½ teaspoons mixed dried herbs

2 medium onions, minced or grated

560 grams whole-wheat flour

20 grams fresh yeast

1 teaspoon sugar

1⅛ cup warm water

½ cup milk

60 grams butter

1½ teaspoons salt

- Crumble yeast into a cup and sprinkle with the sugar. Add two tablespoons of warm water and mix until smooth. Set in a warm place for ten minutes, or until the mixture becomes frothy.
- Pour the milk into a non-stick pan and heat gently. Remove from heat just before the milk begins to boil. Chop the butter, drop into the milk and add the remaining warm water. Set aside for ten minutes, or until the butter has completely melted and the milk remains lukewarm.
- Mix together the flour, salt, herbs and onions. Make a well in the centre and add the yeast mixture and the milk-butter mixture. Knead lightly to make soft dough. Cover with a damp cloth and set aside in a warm place for two hours, or until the dough has doubled in size.
- Grease two baking tins. Knead the dough once again and divide into two portions. Shape the dough into loaves and place in the tins. Cover and set aside for forty-five minutes or until the dough is almost double in size.
- Preheat an oven to180°C/350°F/Gas Mark 4. Place the loaf tins in the oven and bake for forty-five minutes. Increase the heat to 220°C/425°F/Gas Mark 7, and bake for another twenty minutes.
- Remove the loaves from the tins and cool on a wire rack. Slice and serve fresh and warm.

Spicy Pinwheels

1 unsliced bread loaf

6 tablespoons sandwich spread

6 tablespoons chhunda

- Slice the bread horizontally into four slices. Remove the crusts from all the sides.
- Place each bread slice on the worktop. Spread one and a half tablespoons of sandwich spread and one and a half tablespoons of chhunda evenly on it.
- Roll up each bread slice and wrap it up tightly in a cling film. Refrigerate the rolls for fifteen to twenty minutes.
- Cut the bread roll into one-inch thick rounds and serve immediately.

Chef's Tip: You can replace the chhunda with any spicy chutney.

Bread Pakora with Chhunda

8 slices white bread

8 tablespoons chhunda

1½ cups gram flour

¼ teaspoon turmeric powder

1 teaspoon red chilli powder

½ teaspoon carom seeds

Salt to taste

A pinch of soda bicarbonate

2-3 tablespoons rice flour

2 tablespoons chopped fresh coriander

Oil for deep-frying

2 teaspoons Chaat Masala (page 95)

- Arrange four bread slices on a flat surface and spread two tablespoons of chhunda on each of them.
- Cover them with the remaining slices and cut each into four triangles.
- Combine the gram flour, turmeric powder, chilli powder, carom seeds, salt, soda bicarbonate, rice flour and chopped coriander in a bowl.
- Add water, little by little, and mix well to make a smooth batter, without any lumps.

- Heat sufficient oil in a kadai. Dip each bread triangle in the batter and slide it into the hot oil. Deep-fry till golden brown and crisp on both sides.
- Drain on absorbent paper. Sprinkle the chaat masala on them and serve hot.

Nutella Toast

8 tablespoons Nutella

16 slices brown bread

24 walnut kernels, roasted and chopped

- Cut the bread into round slices with a round cookie cutter. Heat a non-stick tawa and toast the bread, turning sides, till both sides are crisp.
- Apply Nutella evenly on all the bread slices. Sprinkle the chopped walnuts on eight slices, cover them with the remaining eight slices. Serve.

Wine Biscuits

100 grams butter

½ cup caster sugar

1 egg white, beaten

¾ cup refined flour

½ teaspoon vanilla essence

- Preheat the oven to 190°C/375°F/Gas Mark 5. Grease a baking tray.
- Cream the butter and caster sugar in a bowl. Add the egg white, a little at a time and continue to cream till all of it is used up. Add the flour and mix well. Add the vanilla essence and mix well.
- Spoon the batter into a piping bag fitted with a star nozzle and pipe one-inch rounds onto the greased baking tray.
- Bake for fifteen minutes or till the top turns a light golden brown. Remove from the oven and transfer the biscuits to a wire rack to cool. Store in an airtight tin.

Bruschetta

1 loaf bread with a hard crust

8-10 garlic cloves, chopped

4 tablespoons butter

3 large tomatoes, seeded and chopped

5-6 fresh basil leaves, shredded

1 tablespoon olive oil

Salt to taste

5-6 black peppercorns, crushed

- Preheat the oven to 180°C/350°F/Gas Mark.
- Cut the loaf diagonally into half-inch thick slices. Mix half the garlic with butter and spread thickly on the slices. Toast the slices in the oven till crisp.
- In a bowl, mix together tomatoes, three-fourth of the shredded basil leaves, olive oil, remaining garlic, salt and crushed peppercorns.
- Rest the mixture for about half an hour. Spread the mixture over the toasted bread and serve, garnished with remaining fresh basil leaves.

Chocolate Danish

8 tablespoons chopped dark chocolate

2¾ cups refined flour + ¼ cup for layering + for dusting

1½ teaspoons salt

2 tablespoons milk powder

2 tablespoons fresh yeast

1 tablespoon sugar

1¼ cups butter

Milk, as required

- Sift together the flour, salt and milk powder into a bowl. Dissolve the yeast and sugar in two tablespoons lukewarm water in another small bowl.
- Add the yeast mixture and one-fourth cup butter to the flour mixture. Add sufficient water and knead into a medium-hard dough.
- Flatten the dough slightly, wrap in cling film and chill for an hour in the refrigerator. To make the butter layering, cream one cup butter till smooth. Add one-fourth cup flour and mix well.
- Dust a silicon sheet with some flour or line an eight-inch rectangular tray with butter paper. Place the butter mixture on it and shape it into a rectangle. Refrigerate for

an hour or till it is almost hard. Remove the dough from the refrigerator and roll it into a rectangle at least three times the size of the butter rectangle.

- Place the butter rectangle in the centre of the rolled out dough, fold over the two smaller sides first and then fold over the two longer sides and seal well to enclose the butter entirely. Ensure that the butter is not too hard while placing it on the dough. Wrap in cling film and keep it in the refrigerator for fifteen to twenty minutes.
- Remove from the refrigerator and roll out into a half-inch thick, seven-inch by five-inch rectangle. Give it a threefold - first fold one-third of the longer side of the rectangle, then fold over the rest to overlap the first fold to make a rectangle again. Wrap in cling film and refrigerate again for half an hour. Remove from the refrigerator and repeat the above process. Wrap in cling film. Refrigerate again for half an hour.
- Remove from the refrigerator and roll out into half inch thickness. Cut into three-inch squares. Place a little chopped chocolate in the centre of each square, apply a little water on the edges and join the diagonally opposite corners to make a triangle.
- Arrange the prepared chocolate danish on a greased baking tray, cover with a damp piece of muslin and allow them to prove for twenty to twenty-five minutes.

- Preheat the oven to 180°C/350°F/Gas Mark 4.
- Uncover the tray and apply a milk wash on the triangles. Bake in the preheated oven for twenty minutes or till light golden in colour. Serve hot.

Spiral Herb Bread

2½ cups refined flour

1½ cups whole-wheat flour

13 grams fresh yeast

1 tablespoon sugar

1½ teaspoons salt

2-3 garlic cloves, chopped

2 spring onions with greens, chopped

2 tablespoons fresh coriander, chopped

3-4 black peppercorns, crushed

15 grams butter

- Combine the yeast with sugar and one-fourth cup lukewarm water, stir and set aside for ten to fifteen minutes to froth.

- Sift the flours and salt into a large bowl. Make a well in the centre and pour in the yeast mixture and approximately one-and-a-half cups of water and mix into a rough dough.
- Transfer the dough to a floured surface and knead until smooth and elastic. Return to the bowl, cover with a damp cloth and leave for about two hours until double in size.
- Knock back the dough; add the garlic, spring onions with greens, chopped coriander and peppercorns and knead well.
- Divide the dough into two equal portions and roll each portion into a cylinder. Twist the two rolls to form a spiral.
- Cover with a damp cloth and set aside to prove till it doubles in size.
- Preheat the oven to 200°C/400°F/Gas Mark 6. Grease a baking tray.
- Place the bread on the baking tray and bake for forty-five minutes till golden brown and soft to the touch. Remove from the oven and brush with melted butter. Transfer to a wire rack to cool. Cut into slices and serve.

Mawa Cupcakes

1½ tablespoons mawa, crumbled

150 grams butter, softened

¾ cup powdered sugar

5 tablespoons milk powder

1½ cups refined flour

2 tablespoons cornflour

1 teaspoon baking powder

1 teaspoon soda bicarbonate

¼ teaspoon green cardamom powder

¼ cup buttermilk

2 tablespoons milk

- Preheat the oven to 180°C/350°F/Gas Mark 4.
- Grease twelve moulds or paper cups. Cream the butter and powdered sugar in a bowl with a wooden spoon till light and fluffy.
- Sift the milk powder into the bowl and continue to mix.

- Add the mawa and mix again. Sift the flour, cornflour, baking powder, soda bicarbonate and cardamom powder together into the bowl and mix. Add buttermilk to adjust the consistency. If the batter is still too thick add a little milk and mix.
- Pour the batter into greased cake moulds or paper cups. Tap the moulds lightly to level the batter. Bake for thirty minutes. Remove from the oven and place on a wire rack to cool before unmoulding. Serve warm or cold.

Chocolate Shrewsbury Biscuits

½ cup dark chocolate chips

½ cup butter

½ cup + 3 tablespoons caster sugar

2 egg yolks

A few drops of vanilla essence

1 ½ cups refined flour

1 teaspoon lemon rind

- Beat the butter and caster sugar in a bowl till light and creamy. Add the egg yolks and mix well. Add the vanilla essence and mix well.
- Sift the flour directly into the butter mixture. Combine gently and knead into a soft dough.
- Add the lemon rind and mix well. Wrap the dough in cling film and refrigerate for thirty to forty minutes.
- Preheat the oven to 180°C/350°F/Gas Mark 4.
- Divide the dough into sixteen equal portions and shape into balls. Sprinkle chocolate chips on each.
- Flatten the balls lightly on your palm and arrange the cookies on a greased baking tray, keeping sufficient distance between them.
- Place the tray in the preheated oven and bake for twenty to twenty-five minutes. Remove from oven and let the biscuits cool down to room temperature.
- Serve or store in an airtight container.

Sprout Cutlet

½ cup sprouted white peas, boiled

½ cup sprouted brown Bengal gram, boiled

½ cup sprouted green Bengal gram, boiled

2 tablespoons finely chopped fresh coriander

Salt to taste

½ teaspoon red chilli powder

½ teaspoon Chaat Masala (page 95)

½ teaspoon cumin powder

Oil for shallow-frying

½ cup breadcrumbs

- Combine the chopped coriander, white peas, brown Bengal gram, green Bengal gram and salt in a bowl. Mash well with a potato masher. Add the red chilli powder, chaat masala and cumin powder and mix well.
- Heat a little oil in a non-stick pan. Divide the sprout mixture into eight portions and shape them into small cutlets, roll them in breadcrumbs and place on the pan. Shallow-fry till the underside is done, flip over and cook till both the sides are evenly golden. Serve hot with tomato ketchup or Green Chutney (page 95).

Bhakarwadi

1 cup refined flour

¾ cup gram flour

Salt to taste

¼ teaspoon turmeric powder

1 teaspoon red chilli powder

1 tablespoon oil + for deep-frying

Stuffing

¼ cup poppy seeds

¼ cup sesame seeds

½ cup grated dried coconut

1 tablespoon finely chopped ginger

3 green chillies, chopped finely

½ tablespoon coriander powder

½ tablespoon cumin powder

2 teaspoons red chilli powder

½ teaspoon turmeric powder

¼ teaspoon asafoetida

2 tablespoons finely chopped fresh coriander

Salt to taste

- Mix together the refined flour, gram flour and salt in a bowl. Add the turmeric powder, chilli powder and one tablespoon oil. Add sufficient water and knead into stiff dough. Cover with a damp cloth and set aside.
- Dry-roast the poppy seeds, sesame seeds and dried coconut separately in a non-stick pan and transfer into a plate and let them cool.
- In another bowl, mix ginger, green chillies, coriander powder, cumin powder, chilli powder and turmeric powder. Add roasted spices and mix well. Add asafoetida, chopped fresh coriander and salt. Grind the entire mixture coarsely.
- Divide the dough into eight equal portions. Roll out each portion into thin rounds. Apply some water on the surface and spread a portion of the stuffing mixture. Roll into cylinders.
- Heat sufficient water in steamer. Place the cylinders on a perforated plate and fit it into the steamer. Steam for twelve to fifteen minutes. Cool the cylinders slightly and cut into half-inch pieces. They can be cut into pieces before steaming too.
- Heat sufficient oil in a kadai and deep-fry the pieces on medium heat till golden brown and crisp. Drain on absorbent paper. Cool and serve. Or store in an air-tight container.

Patra

12 colocasia leaves

1½ cups gram flour

2 teaspoons coriander powder

1 teaspoon cumin powder

1 teaspoon red chilli powder

1 teaspoon turmeric powder

2 teaspoons sesame seeds

Salt to taste

1 teaspoon green chilli paste

1 teaspoon ginger paste

4 tablespoons oil

2 tablespoons tamarind pulp

3½ tablespoons grated jaggery

1 teaspoon mustard seeds

A pinch of asafoetida

¼ cup grated coconut

4 tablespoons chopped fresh coriander

- Remove the thick stems from the colocasia leaves. Wash the leaves, wipe them dry and set aside. Mix together the gram flour, coriander powder, cumin powder, chilli powder and turmeric powder in a bowl. Add the sesame seeds, salt, green chilli paste, ginger paste and two tablespoons of oil, and mix well. Mix together the tamarind pulp and jaggery, and add to the gram flour mixture.

- Place a leaf, shiny side down, on a work surface. Spread the paste evenly over the back of the leaf. Place another leaf over it, with its tapering end in the opposite direction of the irst one. Spread some paste over it.
- Fold in the four edges and gently roll into a tight cylinder. Repeat the same with the rest of the leaves and paste. Place the rolls on a perforated plate or a sieve.
- Heat some water in a pressure cooker and place a metal ring or trivet in it. Place the sieve on the ring and seal the cooker with the lid.
- Steam without the weight for about twenty-five to thirty minutes, or till cooked. Insert a thin knife into the patra to check for doneness. If the knife comes out clean, the patra is cooked. Remove the patra and leave to cool. Cut into quarter-inch thick slices.
- Heat the remaining oil in a non-stick kadai; add the mustard seeds. When they begin to splutter, add the asafoetida and the slices of patra. Sauté till golden brown. Serve hot, garnished with coconut and chopped coriander.

Golden Bags

30 five-inch round spring roll wrappers

1 cup crumbled cottage cheese

½ cup minced mixed vegetables (cauliflower, French beans and green peas)

1 tablespoon chopped fresh coriander

¼ teaspoon black pepper powder

Salt to taste

2 tablespoons oil + for deep-frying

10 garlic cloves, chopped

A few spring onion greens

½ cup sweet chilli sauce

- To make the filling, mix together the cottage cheese, vegetables, chopped coriander, pepper powder and salt.
- Heat two tablespoons of oil in a non-stick wok; add the garlic and sauté until fragrant. Add the cottage cheese mixture and stir-fry for three to four minutes.
- Place one tablespoon of the filling in the centre of each spring roll wrapper, and gather the edges together in pleats to make a bag (potli). Tie the bag

tightly around the filling with a strip of spring onion green stalk. Trim the excess wrapper and spring onion.

- Heat sufficient oil in a wok and deep-fry the bags until golden. Drain on absorbent paper. Serve hot with sweet chilli sauce.

Banana Wafers

4 medium unripe nendra bananas

1 tablespoon oil

Coconut oil for deep-frying

4 teaspoons salt

- Grease your palms with one tablespoon oil. This makes it easy for you to handle and peel the bananas as the skin gives out a resin which is very sticky.
- Peel all the bananas with a peeler and set them aside.

- Heat sufficient coconut oil in a kadai on medium heat. Holding a good quality, heat resistant vegetable slicer over the hot oil, thinly slice one banana directly into the oil. Deep-fry till the wafers become light yellow in colour.
- Mix one teaspoon salt in one tablespoon water in a bowl. Sprinkle this mixture over the oil and wait till the water evaporates.
- Drain the wafers on absorbent paper. Make more wafers with the remaining three bananas in the same manner.
- Serve or cool and store in an air-tight container.

Chef's Tip: Nendra bananas are the big yellow skinned bananas, a speciality of coastal Kerala. The wafers are yellow in colour but no turmeric powder is added. As they get fried they automatically turn yellow. If you do not like the flavour of coconut oil use any other oil of your choice but the flavour will be different.

Mixed Veg Pao

1½ cups refined flour

1½ teaspoons dried yeast

1 teaspoon sugar

1 teaspoon salt

1 tablespoon oil

Filling

2 medium green capsicums, finely chopped

8-10 French beans, finely chopped

2 medium carrots, finely chopped

½ small cabbage, finely chopped

4-6 garlic cloves, finely chopped

2 spring onions, finely chopped

½ teaspoon white pepper powder

Salt to taste

1 teaspoon light soy sauce

- Mix the yeast with one-fourth cup of warm water and sugar in a bowl and set aside until frothy.

- Mix together the refined flour, salt and oil in a bowl. Add the yeast mixture and approximately half a cup of water and knead into a soft dough.
- Cover the dough with a damp cloth and rest in a warm place to rise for about forty-five minutes, or until the dough is approximately double in size. Knock back the dough; cover with a damp cloth again, and leave to stand for ten to fifteen minutes.
- For the filling, mix together the garlic, spring onions, capsicums, French beans, carrots, cabbage, white pepper powder, salt and soy sauce in a bowl.
- Divide the dough into eight equal portions and shape them into balls. Roll the balls into five-inch discs. Place a spoonful of the filling in the centre of each, gather the edges and seal the edges well so that the filling is well enclosed.
- Shape them into balls again and set aside to rest for ten minutes. Heat sufficient water in a steamer. Line a plate with a clean, damp piece of muslin and arrange the paos on it. Place the plate in the steamer, cover the steamer and steam until the paos are cooked through.
- Transfer onto a serving plate and serve hot with Sichuan sauce.

Savoury Crispies with Creamy Onion Dip

2 pita breads

Onion Dip

2 medium onions, sliced

Oil for deep-frying

¾ cup mayonnaise

2 tablespoons fresh cream

1 stalk spring onion greens, chopped

Salt to taste

1 teaspoon black peppercorns, crushed

- Slice the pita bread horizontally and cut again into long triangular slices.
- Heat a tawa and arrange the pita slices on it. Toast both sides over a low heat till crisp.
- Heat sufficient oil in a kadai and deep-fry the onions till golden brown. Drain on absorbent paper. Crush the fried onions lightly.

- Combine the mayonnaise, cream, spring onion greens, salt, crushed peppercorns and browned onions.
- Place in a refrigerator to chill for half an hour. Serve the pita crispies with the onion dip.

Crusty Potato Fingers

2 large potatoes

Salt to taste

2½ cups cornflakes, crushed

Oil for deep-frying

Batter

1 onion, roughly chopped

1 green chilli, chopped

½ inch ginger

Salt to taste

½ cup refined flour

1 tablespoon cornflour

- For the batter, grind the onion, green chilli, ginger and salt to a fine paste.
- Mix the ground paste with the flour and cornflour. Add two tablespoons of water to make a thick batter.
- Peel and cut the potatoes lengthways into even strips. Heat four cups of water in a non-stick pan. Add the salt and parboil the sliced potatoes. Drain and set aside.
- Heat sufficient oil in a kadai. Dip the potatoes in the batter, roll in crushed cornflakes and deep-fry till golden. Drain on absorbent paper.
- Serve hot, with sauce or chutney.

Note: You can also cut the potatoes into large cubes. In which case, serve them on toothpicks.

Mini Falafel Burgers

1 cup chickpeas, soaked overnight

2-3 garlic cloves, chopped

2 tablespoons chopped fresh coriander

2 tablespoons chopped fresh parsley (ajmoda)

4-5 stalks spring onion greens, chopped

¼ cup breadcrumbs

A small pinch of soda bicarbonate

½ teaspoon roasted cumin powder

Salt to taste

¼ teaspoon black pepper powder

½ teaspoon paprika

Oil for deep-frying

Yogurt Sauce

½ cup drained (hung) yogurt

2 tablespoons cream

1 tablespoon chopped fresh coriander

3-4 garlic cloves, chopped

1 teaspoon chopped fresh parsley (ajmoda)

Salt to taste

½ tablespoon lemon juice

To Serve

8 mini burger buns

1 medium cucumber, sliced into ribbons

Butter, as required

4 lettuce leaves, halved
2 cheese slices, quartered
1 medium cucumber, sliced
1 large tomato, sliced

- Drain the chickpeas and spread on a kitchen towel to dry. Process the chickpeas along with garlic, coriander, parsley, spring onion greens and breadcrumbs in a food processor to a coarse mixture.
- Add the soda bicarbonate and cumin powder and mix well. Season with salt, pepper and paprika.
- Knead the mixture well and place in a refrigerator to chill for a couple of hours. Shape tablespoonful of the chilled mixture into round patties.
- Arrange on a greased plate and place in a refrigerator till ready to fry.
- Heat sufficient oil in a kadai and deep-fry the falafels till golden brown. Drain on absorbent paper.

- For the yogurt sauce, mix together all the ingredients for the yogurt sauce and chill till required.
- Apply salt to the cucumber ribbons and set aside. Cut the burger buns in half and spread the cut sides with butter. On the bottom half of each bun place a lettuce leaf, a quartered cheese slice, cucumber slice and tomato slice.
- Place a fried falafel on the vegetable slices and top with yogurt sauce and cucumber ribbons. Cover with the top half of the bun. Serve immediately.

Chef's Tip: In place of mini burgers you can also use small round buns.

Note: *A great hit with kids and adults alike! The yogurt sauce can be served separately as a dip with a variety of crudités so you can make large batches of it.*

Cheese Balls

3 cups cheese spread

¾ cup refined flour

A pinch of salt

75 grams butter

3 eggs

2 teaspoons red chilli flakes

2 teaspoons mixed dried herbs

10-12 black peppercorns, crushed

- Preheat the oven to 200°C/400°F/Gas Mark 6. Grease a baking tray.
- Sift the flour with salt. Place the butter and one cup of water in a non-stick pan and stir over low heat until the butter melts.
- Add the flour all at once and stir over medium heat until the mixture forms a ball and leaves the sides of the pan. Transfer the mixture to a bowl and cool slightly.
- Beat in the eggs, one at a time, until the mixture is smooth and shiny.

- Spoon the mixture into a pastry bag fitted with a plain nozzle. Pipe small mounds onto a baking tray. Bake for twenty to twenty-five minutes or until puffed up and golden brown.
- Make a small hole in the base of the puffs with the tip of a knife or a skewer to allow the steam to escape. Return the puffs to the oven and bake for two more minutes to dry out the insides. Remove from the oven and set aside to cool.
- Combine the cheese spread, chilli flakes, dried herbs and crushed peppercorns and mix well.
- Spoon into a small pastry bag with a plain nozzle and pipe the cheese mixture into the puffs through the hole in the base. Serve immediately.

Egg Mayo Sandwich

4 eggs, boiled, peeled and grated

3 tablespoons mayonnaise

8 slices white bread

A few iceberg lettuce leaves, shredded

1 medium onion, finely chopped

3-4 fresh parsley sprigs, chopped

Black pepper powder to taste

2 tablespoons grated processed cheese

- Place the eggs, lettuce, onion, fresh parsley, pepper powder, cheese and mayonnaise in a bowl and mix well.
- Arrange four bread slices on the work top. Spread a thick layer of the egg-mayo mixture on each. Cover each of them with the remaining bread slices.
- Trim the edges and cut each sandwich into fingers. Serve immediately with tomato ketchup.

Baida Roti

Roti

9 eggs

1 cup refined flour

Salt to taste

1 tablespoon oil

⅛ teaspoon baking powder

Filling

1 tablespoon oil + for shallow-frying

1 medium onion, minced

1 cup minced mutton

2 green chillies, chopped

Salt to taste

¼ teaspoon Garam Masala Powder (page 95)

1 tablespoon chopped fresh coriander

- Mix together the refined flour, salt, oil, baking powder and one egg. Add one-fourth cup of water and knead into soft dough.
- Divide the dough into four equal portions and shape into balls. Cover the dough with a damp piece of muslin and set aside for a few minutes.

- For the filling, heat one tablespoon oil in a non-stick pan, add the onion and sauté till light brown. Add the minced mutton, green chillies and salt and cook over medium heat till the mince is cooked and completely dry. Add the garam masala powder and chopped coriander and mix well.
- Break the remaining eggs into a bowl and beat them well.
- Roll out each dough ball into an eight-inch square chapati.
- Heat a non-stick pan and place the chapati on it. Place some mince mixture in the centre and pour two tablespoons of beaten egg over it. Fold in the sides to make a square package.
- Pour some more beaten egg over and drizzle oil around. Slowly turn the stuffed roti over and pour a little more beaten egg so that the roti is covered with egg on all sides.
- Gently shallow-fry over low heat till both sides are golden and crisp. Drain on absorbent paper. Serve hot with green chutney.

Seafood Spring Rolls

½ cup peeled shrimps

2 (200-250 grams) pomfret fillets, cut into 1-inch pieces

½ cup clams

4 Spring roll wrappers

2 eggs

2 inches ginger, finely chopped

1 teaspoon sesame oil

½ cup thinly sliced spring onions

¼ cup chopped fresh coriander

Salt to taste

10-12 black peppercorns, crushed

Oil for deep-frying

- To make the filling, combine the shrimps, pomfret, clams, one egg, ginger and sesame oil in a food processor.
- Transfer to a large bowl and mix in the spring onions and chopped coriander. Season with salt and crushed peppercorns. Beat the other egg with one-fourth cup of water to make an egg wash.

- For the rolls, place some of the seafood mixture a little below one corner of a spring roll wrapper. Bring in the corners to enclose the filling. Brush the edges with the egg wash, roll tightly towards the middle.
- Heat sufficient oil in a wok. Deep-fry the rolls till golden brown. Drain on absorbent paper. Cut the rolls diagonally into two and serve with Sichuan sauce.

Grilled Fish Fingers

400 grams fish fillet

3 tablespoons lemon juice

4 tablespoons orange juice

Salt to taste

½ teaspoon mustard paste

White pepper powder to taste

A pinch of dried thyme

1 tablespoon Worcestershire sauce

½ cup whole-wheat flour

1 tablespoon oil

- Clean, wash and cut fish fillet into finger-sized pieces. Pat dry with a clean and absorbent kitchen towel.
- Mix together lemon juice, orange juice, salt to taste, mustard paste, white pepper powder, dried thyme and Worcestershire sauce thoroughly.
- Add the fish fingers in the marinade. Refrigerate the marinated fish fingers for about fifteen to twenty minutes.
- Season the flour with salt and white pepper powder.
- Roll marinated fish fingers in seasoned flour. Shake the excess flour off.
- Heat a non-stick tawa; slightly grease with a few drops of oil.
- Place the fish fingers on it. Cook on medium heat, turning it occasionally for uniform cooking and colour. Cook till golden brown in colour.

Chef's Tip: Alternatively, you may cook fish fingers in a preheated oven or a grill.

Golden Fried Jumbo Prawns

12-16 jumbo prawns

4-6 garlic cloves, ground to fine paste

2 tablespoons oyster sauce (optional)

1 tablespoon lemon juice

1 teaspoon soy sauce

½ teaspoon white pepper powder

¼ teaspoon MSG (optional)

Salt to taste

¾ cup refined flour

½ cup cornflour

¼ teaspoon baking powder

¾ cup oil + for deep-frying

- Peel and devein prawns, keeping the shell on the tail intact.
- Mix together garlic paste, oyster sauce, lemon juice, soy sauce, white pepper powder, MSG and salt to taste. Apply this mixture liberally over the prawns; set aside to marinate for two hours, preferably in the refrigerator.
- Mix refined flour, cornflour, baking powder, three-fourth cup oil, salt to taste and three-fourth cup of water.

- Whisk thoroughly to make a batter of pouring consistency; set aside for twenty minutes.
- Heat sufficient oil in a wok. Dip the marinated prawns in the batter and deep-fry for two to three minutes on medium heat, turning frequently, until crisp and golden brown. Remove, drain on absorbent paper. Serve hot with sauce.

Chef's Tip: The batter needs to be whisked thoroughly to incorporate the oil well into the batter. You can increase the quantity of oil in the batter for crispier prawns.

Chicken Cutlet A L' Indienne

4 boneless chicken breasts

1 medium onion, peeled and chopped

2-3 green chillies, chopped

A few sprigs of fresh coriander, chopped

Salt to taste

½ teaspoon black peppercorns, crushed

2 eggs

3 tablespoons fresh cream

1 cup refined flour

1 cup breadcrumbs

½ teaspoon black pepper powder

Oil for shallow-frying

- Wash, clean and mince chicken breasts. In a bowl, mix minced chicken with onion, green chillies, chopped coriander, salt and crushed peppercorns. Set aside for twenty minutes. Beat eggs in a large bowl with the cream. Season the flour and breadcrumbs with salt and pepper powder in separate plates. Set aside.
- Divide the minced chicken into equal portions and shape the chicken into round, oval, heart or pear–shaped cutlets. Coat the cutlets with the seasoned flour, shaking off excess flour, dip into the cream and egg mixture and finally coat with the seasoned breadcrumbs.
- Heat the oil in a non-stick frying pan and shallow-fry the cutlets on both sides, on medium heat till golden brown. Drain on absorbent paper and serve hot.

Mince Hot Dog Rolls

350 grams minced chicken

4 hot dog rolls

1 tablespoon ginger-garlic-green chilli paste

2 tablespoons cashew nut paste

1 teaspoon Chaat Masala (page 95)

1 teaspoon Garam Masala Powder (page 95)

1 teaspoon white pepper powder

4 tablespoons chopped fresh coriander

1 tablespoon lemon juice

Salt to taste

2 tablespoons oil

2 tablespoons butter

1 head of lettuce, shredded

2 medium onions, chopped

4 tablespoons Mint Chutney (page 95)

- Place the minced chicken in a bowl. Add the ginger-garlic-green chilli paste, cashew nut paste, chaat masala, garam masala powder, pepper powder, chopped coriander, lemon juice and salt. Mix well and divide into four portions.

- Moisten your hands, take each portion of the chicken mixture and press it firmly around a satay stick.
- Heat a non-stick tawa and drizzle some oil on it.
- Place the satay sticks on the tawa and cook, turning them from time to time so that they cook evenly on all sides. Baste the kababs with butter at regular intervals. Remove when completely cooked and set aside.
- Heat another non-stick tawa. Slit the hot dog rolls without cutting through and roast them on the tawa till slightly crisp.
- Place some lettuce on each hot dog roll. Place a kabab on the lettuce and top it with some onions and mint chutney.
- Press the top of the roll down lightly and serve immediately.

Chicken Flower Dumpling

¾ cup Basmati rice
300 grams minced chicken
2-3 green chillies, finely chopped
1 inch ginger, ground to a paste
Salt to taste
1 teaspoon black peppercorns, crushed

- Soak rice in water for twenty minutes. Drain and set aside.
- Mix chicken with green chillies, ginger paste, salt and crushed peppercorns. Divide this mixture into twelve equal portions. Shape each portion into round balls and roll them in the soaked and drained rice.
- Place chicken balls on a perforated steamer rack. Boil water in the steamer; place the perforated rack in it and cover the pan. Steam for about fifteen to twenty minutes or until cooked. Remove gently and serve hot with a dip of your choice.

Chef's Tip: Chicken Flower Dumplings are best made best with minced chicken that is extra fine, preferably from chicken supremes.

Chicken Calzones

Pastry

2 cups refined flour

½ teaspoon salt

5 grams fresh yeast

½ teaspoon sugar

1 tablespoon olive oil

Butter, as required

Filling

2 chicken breasts, chopped

Salt to taste

3-4 black peppercorns, crushed

2 tablespoons olive oil

4 garlic cloves, chopped

2 medium onions, chopped

1 medium green capsicum, chopped

½ cup Tomato Concasse (page 74)

½ teaspoon red chilli flakes

½ teaspoon dried mixed herbs

1 jalapeño chilli, chopped

- For the pastry, sift the refined flour with salt and make a well in the centre. Dissolve the yeast in lukewarm water along with sugar and pour into the well. Mix.
- Make a soft dough using water as required. Cover with a damp cloth and set aside at room temperature till it doubles in size.
- Preheat the oven to 200°C/400°F/Gas Mark 6. Grease a baking tray with one tablespoon olive oil. Knock back the dough lightly, divide into four equal portions and roll out each portion into a one-inch thick round. Set aside for about twenty minutes in a warm place.
- For the filling, heat the olive oil in a non-stick pan; add the garlic and sauté for one minute. Add the onions and continue to sauté till translucent.
- Add the capsicum and chicken and sauté for three to four minutes. Stir in the tomato concasse and cook till well blended. Add the chilli flakes, mixed herbs, jalapeño chilli, salt and crushed peppercorns.
- Mix well, remove from heat and set aside to cool. Divide the mixture into four portions and spread each portion over a pastry round.

- Fold over into a half-moon shape. Press the edges together to seal and place on the greased tray. Bake for about forty-five minutes till golden brown. Brush with melted butter and serve hot.

Tomato Concassé

To make 1 cup of tomato concassé, blanch 5 medium tomatoes in plenty of boiling water for two minutes. Drain and refresh in cold water; peel, cut in half, remove seeds and chop roughly.

Sausage Triangles

4 sheets filo pastry

200 grams chicken sausages, chopped

2 medium potatoes, boiled and mashed

3 teaspoons oil

1 large onion, grated

2 garlic cloves, chopped

Salt to taste

5-6 black peppercorns, crushed

1 egg, beaten lightly

- Preheat the oven to 220°C/425°F/Gas Mark 7.
- Heat the oil in a small non-stick pan; add the onion and garlic and sauté till translucent. Transfer to a bowl.
- Add the mashed potatoes and sausages and mix well. Add salt and the crushed peppercorns and mix again. Cut each pastry sheet in half.
- Divide the sausage mixture equally among the pastry halves, placing it at one end of the pastry sheet. Brush the beaten egg mixture around the edges and fold into triangles.
- Place the triangles on a lightly oiled baking tray. Bake, uncovered, for about twenty-five minutes, or until lightly browned. Serve hot.

Seekh Roti

Filling

500 grams boneless mutton, cut into 1-inch cubes

4 tablespoons unripe green papaya paste

1 tablespoon garlic paste

½ tablespoon ginger paste

4-5 green chillies, chopped

1 tablespoon red chilli powder

½ tablespoon coriander powder

1 teaspoon roasted cumin powder

1 teaspoon garam masala powder

Salt to taste

3 tablespoons ghee

2 large onions, chopped

1 teaspoon poppy seeds

1 teaspoon sesame seeds

1½ tablespoons vinegar

To Serve

8 roomali rotis

¼ cup Green Chutney (page 95)

2 large onions, sliced

2 tablespoons chopped fresh mint

- In a large bowl, combine the mutton, papaya paste, garlic paste, ginger paste, green chillies, chilli powder, coriander powder, roasted cumin powder, garam masala powder and salt. Leave to marinate for four to five hours, preferably in a refrigerator.
- Heat two tablespoons ghee in a non-stick kadai; add the onion and sauté over medium heat till pale gold. Add the marinated mutton, stir and cook, uncovered, on low heat for ten minutes. Add half a cup of water, cover and cook for twenty to twenty-five minutes or till the mutton is tender. Add the poppy and sesame seeds and continue to cook, uncovered, for another fifteen minutes till all the water has evaporated. Stir in the vinegar, remove from heat and set aside.
- To obtain a smoky flavour, place a live piece of charcoal in a bowl and place the bowl in the centre of the mutton mixture. Pour one tablespoon of hot ghee on the charcoal, cover the pan immediately and leave to stand for three to four minutes. Remove the bowl with the charcoal from the mutton mixture.
- To prepare the wraps, divide the mutton mixture into eight equal portions. Place a roti on a plate and smear some green chutney over it. Spread a portion of the mutton mixture over the roti, sprinkle some sliced onions and fresh mint, roll up into a wrap and secure with a piece of aluminium foil.

Parsi Mutton Cutlets

500 grams minced mutton

5 slices bread

Salt to taste

½ tablespoon ginger paste

½ tablespoon garlic paste

6-8 green chillies, finely chopped

1½ teaspoons red chilli powder

1 teaspoon coriander powder

1 teaspoon roasted cumin powder

¼ teaspoon turmeric powder

2 tablespoons chopped fresh mint

2 tablespoons chopped fresh coriander

1 cup breadcrumbs

Oil for deep-frying

4 eggs

Lemon wedges, as required

Onion rings, as required

- Squeeze the minced mutton between your palms to remove excess water.
- Soak the bread in one cup of water for half a minute and squeeze to remove excess water.

- Place the mutton, bread, salt, ginger paste, garlic paste, green chillies, chilli powder, coriander powder, cumin powder, turmeric powder, chopped fresh mint and coriander in a deep bowl. Mix well and set aside to marinate for three to four hours, preferably in a refrigerator.
- Divide the marinated mince into twelve equal portions; shape each portion into a ball and roll in breadcrumbs. Place each ball on a flat surface and flatten with your fingers into a fou-rinch patty, dusting with breadcrumbs. Place the cutlets in a refrigerator for half an hour.
- Heat sufficient oil in a deep kadai. Beat the eggs lightly with salt and two tablespoons of water. Dip the cutlets in the egg and deep-fry for two to three minutes on each side. Drain on absorbent paper.
- Serve hot with lemon wedges and onion rings.

Note: These cutlets can be made a day ahead and frozen. Place butter paper between the layers and fry as you need them.

Churros with Chocolate Sauce

Choux Paste

¼ cup butter

1 tablespoon caster sugar

¼ teaspoon salt

1 cup refined flour

2 eggs

Oil for deep-frying

Cinnamon Sugar

½ cup caster sugar

1 teaspoon cinnamon powder

Chocolate Sauce

½ cup melted dark chocolate

- To make the choux paste, boil one cup of water in a non-stick pan. Add the butter, caster sugar and salt and cook till the butter melts.
- Add the flour and stir vigorously till the mixture becomes smooth and soft and begins to leave the sides of the pan.

- Take the pan off the heat. Add one egg at a time and keep stirring till the mixture forms a smooth paste.
- Do not over mix. Allow the mixture to cool down to room temperature and refrigerate for fifteen to twenty minutes.
- To make the cinnamon sugar, mix together the caster sugar and cinnamon powder in a bowl and set aside.
- Heat sufficient oil in a kadai.
- Pour choux paste into a piping bag fitted with a plain nozzle and pipe it directly into hot oil, cutting the ends with the help of scissors to get churro pieces of at least two inches in length. Deep-fry till light golden.
- Drain on absorbent paper and roll them in the cinnamon sugar. Ensure that all of them are coated evenly.
- Serve immediately with melted chocolate as a dipping sauce.

Steamed Date Buns

Dough

450 grams refined flour

3 teaspoons sugar

1½ tablespoons dried yeast

½ cup milk

¼ teaspoon salt

1 tablespoon sesame oil

Filling

125 grams seedless dates, finely chopped

1 tablespoon butter

2 tablespoons sweet bean paste

½ cup walnut kernels, finely chopped

- Dissolve the sugar and dried yeast in lukewarm milk and leave aside for fifteen minutes or until frothy.
- Sieve the refined flour and salt together, make a well in the centre, add the yeast mixture and make a soft dough adding enough water.

- Add sesame oil and knead the dough with your palm and set aside in a warm place for fifteen minutes or until it doubles in size. Knock out the air bubbles by kneading once again and divide into sixteen equal portions.
- Heat the butter in a non-stick pan and stir in the bean paste diluted in two tablespoons of water.
- Add the dates and walnuts and cook for two minutes till it starts leaving the sides of the pan. Remove from heat and cool.
- Roll each portion of the dough into two-inch round discs; place a portion of the filling and gather the sides to form into a ball.
- Rest the prepared buns covered with a moist piece of muslin for five minutes. Place in bamboo steamers and steam on high heat for fifteen minutes or until completely cooked. Serve hot straight from the steamer.

Baked Lemon Tart

1 recipe Basic Shortcrust Pastry (page 85)

Juice of 4 lemons

Grated rind of 4 lemons

6 eggs, beaten

1½ cups caster sugar

115 grams unsalted butter

- Preheat the oven to 200°C/400°F/Gas Mark 6.
- Roll out the pastry dough on a lightly floured surface and line one nine-inch tart tin or six two-inch tartlet tins. Prick the pastry all over with a fork.
- Place in a refrigerator for ten minutes. Bake blind in the preheated oven for ten minutes.
- For the filling, place eggs, caster sugar and butter in a non-stick pan and stir over low heat until the sugar has dissolved.

- Add the lemon juice and rind and continue cooking, stirring continuously, until the lemon curd thickens slightly.
- Pour the mixture into the pastry case and bake for twenty minutes, or until the filling is just set.
- Remove from the oven and place on a wire rack to cool. Cut into wedges and serve.

Basic Shortcrust Pastry

Process 1 cup refined flour and 60 grams chilled and chopped butter in a food processor until the mixture resembles coarse breadcrumbs. If mixing by hand, rub the butter into the flour with your fingertips. With the processor running, add drops of iced water until the dough comes together or mix it in with a knife or a wooden spoon or lightly with your fingers. It will need approximately 2½ tablespoons of water. Press the dough into a ball, wrap in greaseproof paper or cling film and refrigerate for at least 30 minutes before rolling or shaping. Makes enough for one 9-inch pastry base.

Note: Shortcrust pastry can be stored in a refrigerator for two days, or in the freezer for up to three months.

Strawberry Panna Cotta

½ cup strawberry crush

1 cup milk

¼ cup sugar

1 tablespoon unflavoured gelatine

2 cups cream

- Boil milk with sugar in a deep non-stick pan. Cool it down to room temperature.
- Soften gelatine in four tablespoons of hot water and stir it into the milk.
- Add the strawberry crush and cream and mix well.
- Pour into eight ramekins (small individual bowls) or moulds and place in a refrigerator to set. Serve chilled.

Sticky Date Pudding

1 cup chopped seedless dates

1 teaspoon soda bicarbonate

6 tablespoons (90 grams) softened butter

½ cup soft brown sugar

2 eggs, lightly beaten

1 teaspoon vanilla essence

1½ cups refined flour

Sauce

6 tablespoons (90 grams) butter

1 cup soft brown sugar

1 cup cream

- Preheat oven to 180⁰C/350⁰F/Gas Mark 4.
- Put dates in a bowl. Heat one cup water in microwave oven and pour over the dates. Add soda bicarbonate and mix and let them soak for fifteen minutes.
- Place butter and brown sugar in a bowl and beat with a hand blender till well blended. Add eggs and beat. Add vanilla essence and beat some more.

- Brush a square dish with butter. Add some flour to butter mixture and mix. Add dates with the water and beat again. Add the remaining flour and mix well.
- Pour the mixture into the prepared tin and bake for fifty minutes or till a skewer inserted into the pudding comes out clean.
- Leave the pudding in the tin to cool for ten minutes before turning out.
- To make the sauce, place the sugar, cream, butter and vanilla essence in a pan and bring to a boil, stirring continuously. Lower the heat and simmer for five minutes.
- Serve the warm pudding with the hot sauce.

Swiss Roll

¾ cup refined flour

½ teaspoon baking powder

4 eggs, separated

¾ cup powdered sugar, sifted

1 teaspoon vanilla essence

¼ teaspoon salt

5 tablespoons mixed fruit jam

2 teaspoons caster sugar, for dusting

- Preheat the oven to 190°C/375°F/Gas Mark 5. Line a fifteen-inch by ten-inch baking tray with greased thick unglazed brown paper.
- Sift the flour together with the baking powder. Beat the egg yolks until light; continue beating the mixture, adding the sugar gradually, till creamy. Stir in the vanilla essence.
- Gently and gradually fold the flour into the egg mixture. Beat the batter until smooth. Whip the egg whites with salt until stiff, but not dry. Fold the egg whites lightly into the cake batter.

- Spread the batter in the prepared tray and bake for about twelve minutes. While still hot, turn the cake out onto a sheet of greaseproof paper, sprinkled with icing sugar.
- Trim the hard edges. Spread the cake with jam and carefully roll it up. Wrap the roll in the butter paper. Cut into slices and serve.

Cream Scones

⅓ cup cream

2 cups refined flour

2¼ teaspoons baking powder

6 measures sucralose

½ teaspoon salt

60 grams chilled butter

2 eggs, beaten

- Preheat the oven to 220°C/450°F/Gas Mark 8.
- Sift the flour, baking powder, sucralose and salt together into a bowl. Cut the butter into the mixture with two knives till the mixture resembles small pellets.
- Reserve two tablespoons of beaten egg; add the cream to the rest of the egg and beat well. Make a well in the centre of the dry ingredients and pour the egg mixture into it. Combine the ingredients with a few swift strokes. Handle the dough as little as possible.
- Place the dough on a lightly floured board and pat it into a three-fourth inch thick round. Cut the dough with a very sharp knife into diamond shapes – each side measuring one-and-a-half inches; or stamp out rounds with a cutter.
- Brush the scones with the reserved beaten egg and sprinkle salt on top. Place on a baking tray and bake for about fifteen minutes.
- Serve warm with jam and cream or butter.

Besan ke Laddoo

4 cups gram flour

12-15 cashew nuts

12-15 almonds

1 cup ghee

1 teaspoon green cardamom powder

2 cups powdered sugar

- Sieve the gram flour through a fine sieve and set aside. Coarsely grind cashew nuts and almonds and set aside. Melt the ghee in a non-stick kadai.
- Add the gram flour and cook on low heat till it is fragrant and well done. This normally takes about fifteen to twenty minutes. Add the cardamom powder, cashew nuts and almonds. Stir and take it off the heat.
- Let it cool for a while. Add the powdered sugar and mix well. You may use your hands to mix this. Shape into walnut-sized round laddoos and store in an air-tight container when completely cooled.

Chef's Tip: While serving Besan Laddoos that have been kept for a few days in the refrigerator, warm them for fifteen to twenty seconds in the microwave. They will not only become soft but also seem freshly made.

Basic Recipes

Chaat Masala

Dry-roast 4 tablespoons coriander seeds, 2 teaspoons cumin seeds and 1 teaspoon carom seeds separately. Cool and powder them with 2-3 whole dried red chillies, 3 tablespoons black salt and ½ teaspoon citric acid. Mix in 1 teaspoon dried mango powder, 1 tablespoon salt and 1 teaspoon white/black pepper powder. Store in an airtight container.

Garam Masala Powder

Dry-roast 10-12 blades mace, 8-10 one-inch cinnamon sticks, 25 cloves, 25 green cardamoms, 10-12 black cardamoms, 2 whole nutmegs, 8-10 bay leaves, 8 teaspoons cumin seeds and 4 teaspoons black peppercorns separately, on a tawa. Cool and grind together all the spices to a fine powder. Store in an airtight jar in a cool, dry place.

Green Chutney

Grind together 1 cup fresh coriander, ½ cup fresh mint, 2-3 green chillies, black salt to taste, ¼ teaspoon sugar and 1 tablespoon lemon juice to a smooth paste using a little water if required.

Glossary

English	Hindi
Almonds	Badam
Asafoetida	Hing
Bay leaf	Tej patta
Bengal gram, brown	Chane
Black gram, skinless, split	Dhuli urad dal
Black peppercorns	Kali mirch
Carom seeds	Ajwain
Caster sugar	Pisi hui shakkar
Chickpeas	Kabuli chana
Cinnamon	Dalchini
Clams	Teesrya
Cloves	Laung
Colocasia	Arbi
Coriander seeds	Sabut dhania
Dried mango powder	Amchur
Fenugreek seeds	Methi dana
French beans	Faras bean
Gram flour	Besan
Mace	Javitri
Nutmeg	Jaiphal
Parsley	Ajmoda
Peas, white	Safed matar
Pomfret	Saranga
Poppy seeds	Khus khus
Raisins	Kishmish
Saffron	Kesar
Semolina	Rawa/ sooji
Shrimps	Jhinga
Vinegar	Sirka
Walnut	Akhrot
Yeast	Khameer
Yogurt	Dahi